RIVET

SPACE HOPPING

The planets as you've never seen them before!

Nigel Henbest

Illustrations by Sebastian Quigley

mammoth

Contents

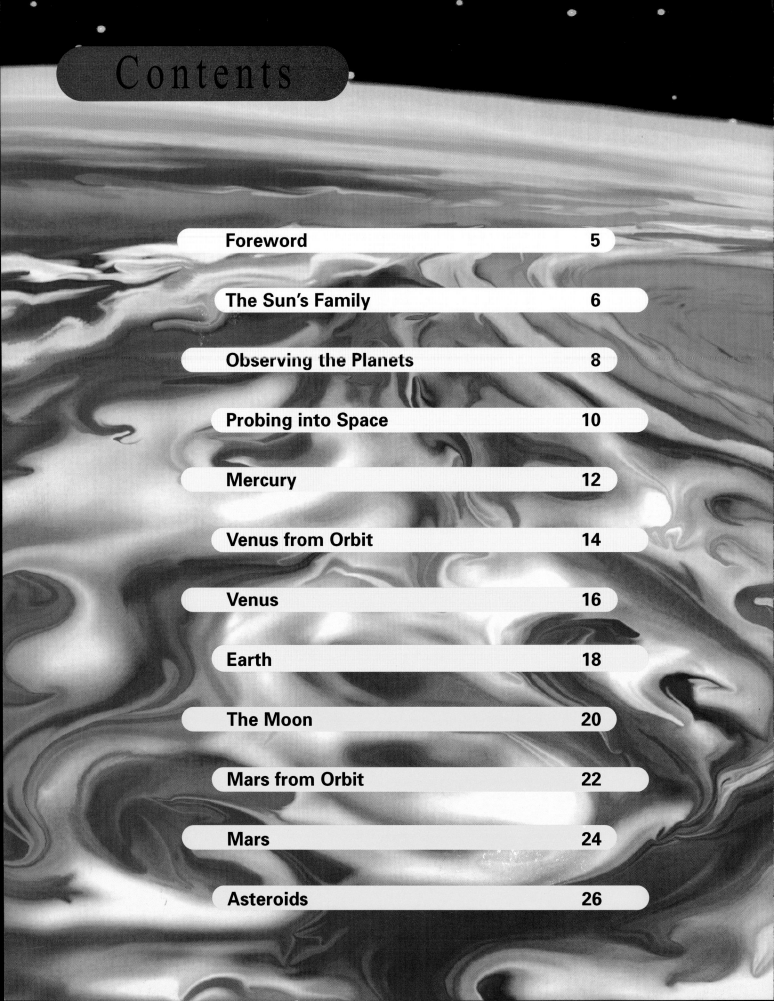

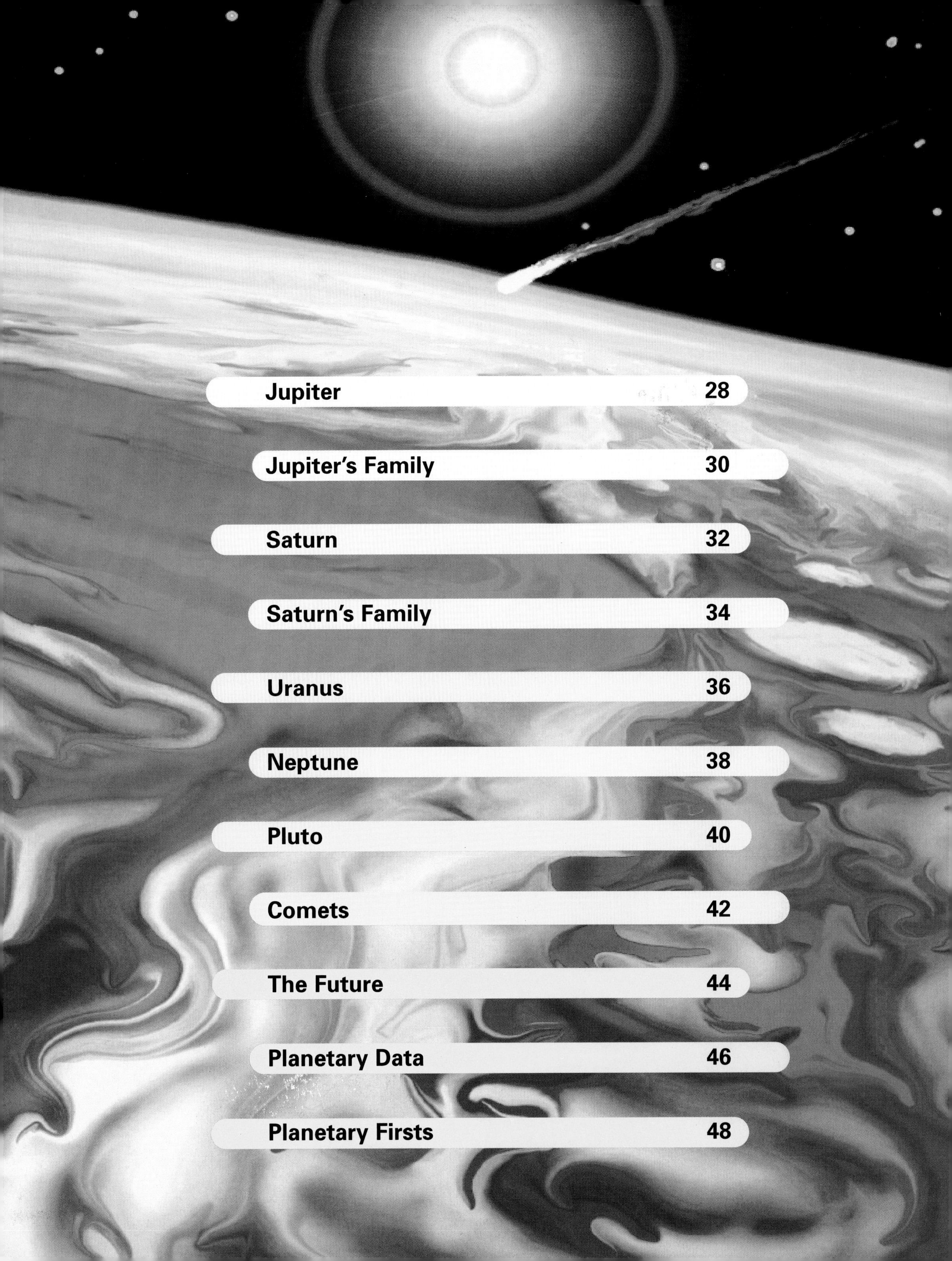

First published in 1999 by Mammoth, an imprint of Egmont Children's Books,
239 Kensington High Street, London W8 6SA

ISBN 0 7497 3997 5

Printed in Hong Kong

A CIP catalogue record for this book is available from the British Library.

Foreword

Imagine you could live on a different planet. Not on the Earth, with its blue sky and green trees, but a world where the sky and the ground are different colours – or where there might not be a ground at all!

The Apollo astronauts experienced an alien world, when they walked on the Moon in the years 1969 to 1972. There was no air, and the sky was so black that they could see stars even during the day. The rocks and soil were a lifeless greyish-brown.

No one has yet been to the other planets circling the Sun – Mercury, Venus, Mars, Jupiter, Saturn, Uranus, Neptune and Pluto. But unmanned spacecraft have now visited most of them, and even landed on some of these planets. They have sent back pictures and measurements that tell astronomers just what these other worlds are like.

Volcanic Venus, for instance, is so hot that its rocks glow in the dark. Giant Jupiter has no surface: anyone who tried to land would just sink downwards through layer after layer of gas.

In this book, we show what it would be like to visit the other planets, their moons – and some stranger celestial objects, like comets.

Happy Space Hopping!

Nigel Henbest

Nigel Henbest

THE *Sun's* FAMILY

Our home in space, planet Earth, is one of nine worlds that orbit the Sun. The Sun is our local star.

The Earth is a fairly average kind of planet. Some planets, like Jupiter and Saturn, are far bigger; while Mercury and Pluto are much smaller. Venus is hotter than the Earth, while distant Pluto is incredibly cold. But there are distinct family characteristics.

OUR SOLAR SYSTEM

All the planets go round the Sun in the same direction, in orbits that are roughly circular. The four planets closest to the Sun – Mercury, Venus, Earth and Mars – are made of rock and have only one or two moons.

Also orbiting within the Sun's powerful gravity are smaller bodies: rocky asteroids, frozen comets and ice dwarfs. These are also members of the Sun's family, known as the Solar System.

STAR QUALITY

The Sun is the undisputed master of our Solar System. It contains almost a thousand times more matter than all the planets put together, and its gravitational pull keeps all the planets in tow. The Sun is so massive that nuclear reactions take place at its core, making it shine. This gives it "star" status.

BIRTH OF THE SOLAR SYSTEM

The Sun and its family of planets were born together 4,600 million years ago, from a giant swirling cloud of gas and "dust" – small pieces of rock, soot and ice. Most of the matter fell to the centre to make the Sun, while the rest formed a whirling disc around it. Close to the Sun's heat, the dust built up into rocky planets. Further out, slivers of ice formed the outer planets: four of them grew into giants by capturing more gas.

JUPITER

VENUS

MERCURY

The four "gas giants":
Jupiter, Saturn, Uranus
and Neptune have
no solid surface,
but are made
of gas or liquid.
They also have
rings and large
families of
moons going
around them.

SATURN

URANUS

NEPTUNE

MARS

PLUTO

EARTH

Observing
the Planets

You can spot most of the planets with your naked eye, but even the world's most powerful telescopes don't reveal all their secrets.

Even if you don't know one star from another, you will sometimes be struck by a "star" more brilliant than any other and that shines with a steady light, rather than twinkling. A few weeks later, it has moved to another part of the sky. The Greeks gave these moving lights in the sky the name *planetes*, meaning "wanderers". Today we call them the planets.

The Italian scientist Galileo Galilei (right) was the first person to study the sky through a telescope, in 1609. Even his simple telescope – no more powerful than modern binoculars – revealed that Jupiter has four moons and that, like the Moon, Venus has changing phases as it goes around the Sun.

Telescopes provide astronomers with a grandstand view of the Universe. They help in two ways. First, a telescope magnifies whatever you are studying so you can see fine details, like the cloud patterns on Jupiter or Mars's dark markings. Second, a telescope makes faint objects look brighter. Neptune, for instance, is invisible to the naked eye but appears as a wonderful bluish globe through a powerful telescope.

If you have a small telescope at home, you can see the Great Red Spot on Jupiter, the rings of Saturn and the phases of Venus. But the professional astronomers of today don't look through telescopes. That would provide only a fleeting view, and the human eye can also be deceived by optical illusions, such as the supposed "canals of Mars" reported by Victorian astronomers. Instead, they record the view through the telescope with an electronic chip, exactly like the chip in a television camera or a home camcorder. They can then show the image on a computer screen, and analyse it at leisure.

But even the most powerful telescopes have a problem. They must look up through the atmosphere, and this is constantly churned by winds. The higher the magnification, the worse the view looks. With a powerful telescope, it's like looking through the water of a busy swimming pool and trying to see the patterns on its floor.

The Hubble Space *Telescope was launched by US and European astronomers in 1990 to give a sharper view on the Universe. From its orbit above Earth's churning atmosphere, the Hubble can use higher magnification on the planets. It has imaged dust storms on Mars, giant white clouds swirling round Saturn and the fiery impact of Comet Shoemaker-Levy-9 on Jupiter.*

If you are studying the planets you need high magnification to see all the intricate details. Because of this, telescopes on Earth are very limited in what they can tell us about even the nearest of our planetary neighbours.

SPOTTING THE PLANETS

The most brilliant planet is Venus, which is covered in dazzling clouds. Because its orbit lies closer to the Sun than the Earth's orbit, it never strays far from the Sun in the sky. You may see it in the west after sunset as the "Evening Star", or in the east before sunrise as the "Morning Star".

Little Mercury, nearest planet to the Sun, never strays out of the twilight glow. It's so difficult to spot that Nicolaus Copernicus, the astronomer who first said that the planets go around the Sun, was never able to see it!

The other planets lie outside the Earth's orbit. When they line up with the Earth, we can see them throughout the night. Mars has a reddish glow; Jupiter is brighter and shines yellowish-white; and Saturn is a dull yellow colour. You need binoculars or a telescope to spot the three outermost planets Uranus, Neptune and tiny Pluto.

Probing *into Space*

In the 1950s, astronomers using telescopes on the Earth thought they knew a lot about the planets. They believed that Venus could have rainforests, that Jupiter's moons were deadly dull, and that primitive vegetation could be growing on Mars.

Then came the Space Age. The Russians launched the first satellite around the Earth in 1957, the first probe to the Moon two years later and the first man in space in 1961. Just a year later, an unmanned American probe made the first visit to another world when Mariner 2 flew past Venus – and found it was far hotter than anyone had expected.

This surprise was the opening shot in a series of new and exciting discoveries as spaceprobes have visited each world. These include giant canyons on Mars, volcanoes on one of Jupiter's moons and thousands of ringlets surrounding Saturn.

Spaceprobes have shown us that just about everything we used to believe about the planets was wrong!

CASSINI
Arriving at Saturn in 2004, it will drop the Huygens lander on to the moon Titan.

ULYSSES
This probe flew past Jupiter so that the giant planet's gravity could flick it upwards and over the Sun's north pole.

PATHFINDER & SOJOURNER
Giant airbags cushioned the USA's Pathfinder when it fell to the surface of Mars in 1997. Its six-wheeled "rover", Sojourner, then trundled out to analyse the surrounding rocks.

AIRBAGS
SURROUNDING
PATHFINDER

SOJOURNER

ULYSSES

PIONEER 10
The first spacecraft to fly through the asteroid belt, it showed that collisions could be avoided – and sent back close-ups of Jupiter.

PIONEER 10

MARINER 10
This craft flew past Venus in 1974 before becoming the first, and so far only, probe to visit Mercury. Its power came from solar panels that converted sunlight to electricity.

MARINER 10

VENERA
A series of heavily armoured Venera craft landed on Venus's hostile surface, sending pictures back to Russia for about an hour before succumbing to the heat and pressure.

VOYAGER 2
Between its launch in 1977 and 1989, Voyager 2 made an epic trip past all four "gas giants", sending back detailed views of the planets and their rings and moons. Too far from the Sun to generate power from solar cells, it carried small nuclear generators.

VIKING

VOYAGER 2

VENERA

VIKING
From orbit round Mars in 1976, two Viking Orbiters sent back detailed views of volcanoes and canyons below. They also dropped two landers, which searched for signs of life.

Mercury

An airless and battered world, Mercury is baked by the Sun on one side and chilled by the cold of space on the other.

Closer to the Sun than any other planet, Mercury feels the full force of the Sun's heat. The midday temperature soars to 430°C, hot enough to melt lead and boil the other mercury – the one found in a thermometer.

But this small world has no air to hold the heat in. Without the covering "blanket" of an atmosphere, the temperature at night plummets to minus 180°C. Such a low temperature on Earth would condense our atmosphere into a liquid!

If you visited Mercury, you would need extra stamina to endure these conditions. A whole day, from sunrise to sunrise, lasts for 176 Earth-days.

Without an atmosphere to scatter the Sun's light, the sky above Mercury is black and filled with stars even during the day.

The depths of this crater, near the planet's pole, are always in shadow. This probably preserves drifts of ice and snow – even on the closest planet to the Sun!

Mariner 10, the only spaceprobe to visit Mercury, found that its surface is pitted everywhere with huge craters, blasted out by giant rocks from space.

DAILY BIRTHDAYS

Mercury is so close to the Sun that it whirls round much faster than the Earth. One complete orbit – a Mercury "year" – takes only 88 Earth-days, only half the length of a Mercury day. So on Mercury you would have two birthdays each day!

A BALL OF IRON

Although tiny Mercury is not much bigger than our Moon, it is much heavier. So it must be made of material that is more dense than common Earth rocks. Astronomers believe the surface rocks we can see there are covering an interior made mainly of iron, which is a very dense metal. Electric currents flow through this iron interior, generating a magnetic field that is surprisingly strong for such a small world – more powerful than the magnetism of Venus or Mars.

Venus *from Orbit*

The brightest and most beautiful planet in our night skies, Venus has long kept its secrets hidden.

Venus comes closer to the Earth than any other planet, yet until the Space Age no one knew what it was like at all. Different theories claimed that it was covered with water, coated in oil or alive with rainforests. Even the most powerful telescopes on Earth gave no clues, because they could not see through the thick clouds which envelop Venus.

The first clues came from radar. Just as the radar used at an airport can detect incoming planes even through clouds or mist or fog, astronomers can use radar to peer through Venus's cloud layers. In the 1960s, very powerful radar sets on Earth started to "strip" Venus bare.

A VERY LONG DAY

The radar views showed how slowly Venus is spinning – and this came as a huge surprise. Venus rotates once in 243 Earth-days, more slowly than any other planet. And it spins in the opposite direction to all the other planets: if you stood on Venus, and could strip the clouds away, you'd see the Sun rise in the West and set in the East.

Since 1978, spaceprobes orbiting Venus have been peering through the clouds from close quarters. Although it is virtually the Earth's twin in size, radar reveals that the two worlds are totally different. Venus is dry, hot and volcanic.

The pale yellow clouds *covering the whole of Venus are not made of water droplets: they are composed of sulphuric acid emitted from volcanoes far below. Drops from the clouds may fall on the planet as highly corrosive acid rain.*

With radar, you can make the clouds seem transparent – and see the surface of the planet below.

Message from Magellan: the radar set carried in 1990 by the American spaceprobe Magellan has sent back the most detailed views of Venus.

Venus

It's the nearest place we know to Hell – a scorched volcanic planet shrouded in poisonous gases.

No astronauts have landed on Venus, and none would ever want to. The first spacecraft to venture there were destroyed by heat and pressure in the atmosphere before they even got down to the surface. So Russian scientists built tougher and tougher spaceprobes, and in 1975 *Venera 9* was successful in landing on Venus's surface. It sent back pictures for a few minutes before it was defeated by the intense pressure and searing heat.

NIGHTMARE PLANET

The images showed bare rocks that were hot enough to glow in the dark: *Venera 9* had landed on the flanks of a volcano. But, as it turned out, the scene would be much the same anywhere on Venus, since the whole planet is a volcanic nightmare. It is estimated to have over 100,000 volcanoes, together with lava streams and giant pools of molten rock. In some places, thick lava has oozed out to make round, flat "rock pancakes" as large as a city; in other places, the surface has split into cracks that look like giant spiders.

Venus is the only planet named after a goddess, and astronomers have given almost all of its mountains, valleys and canyons female names. You can find a crater called Cleopatra, a plain named after Helen of Troy, a giant canyon named Diana and a bright marking called Eve.

Venusian "air" consists of gas belched out from the volcanoes. Made up mainly of unbreathable carbon dioxide, it is 90 times denser than the Earth's atmosphere. Carbon dioxide traps the Sun's heat like a greenhouse, taking temperatures to 470°C.

Some streams of molten lava are as long as the Earth's longest rivers.

Lava from the volcanoes is constantly covering up the older rocks around them. As a result, all of Venus's exposed surface is quite recent – less than a tenth of the age of the Earth's oldest rocks.

If you were unwise enough to land on Venus – with its thick carbon dioxide atmosphere, acid rain and extremely high temperatures – you would be crushed, suffocated, corroded and roasted all at the same time!

EARTH

In many ways, ours is the most unusual planet of all . . .

If you approached the Solar System from space, one planet would stand out as very odd. The third world from the Sun is brightly coloured, in shades of mainly blue, with patches of red and green, and constantly shifting patterns of white cloud. And it has an unusually large moon, which – by contrast – is dull and uniformly brown.

THE PERFECT PLANET

Come closer, and you find the blue is liquid water. This is the only rocky planet with water (though Uranus and Neptune further out are made largely of water right through). Test the atmosphere, and again this planet is unique: the air contains a lot of the reactive gas oxygen. And finally, take a close look at the green areas. Here there is ample vegetation (which is producing the oxygen), and animal life. This is the only planet in the Solar System obviously inhabited by lifeforms.

The Earth is special mainly because it is located at the perfect distance from the Sun. The temperature here is just right for water to exist as a liquid: get in as close as Venus and the water boils away as steam, while as far out as the orbit of Mars water is frozen to ice.

Soon after its birth, the Earth was a very different place from the one we know today. Its "air" was made of the unbreathable and poisonous gases we still find on other planets, such as carbon dioxide and hydrogen cyanide. Comets fell from the sky as giant fireballs, and lethal ultraviolet light rays from the Sun irradiated the surface.

In all this mayhem, simple chemicals from the air and the infalling comets dissolved in the oceans. They gradually joined together in a "primordial soup" to make the first living cells.

LIFE ON EARTH

Life became an important force in shaping the environment. The first plant cells in the sea took in carbon dioxide from the air, and gave out oxygen by the process of photosynthesis. Animals emerged which could breathe the oxygen. And some of the oxygen turned into an ozone layer high in the atmosphere that shielded the surface from the harmful ultraviolet rays of the Sun. Lifeforms emerged on to dry land, evolving into the familiar variety of plants and animals we know today.

The Moon

Our close companion in space – the Moon – is the only place beyond Earth where astronauts have walked.

The explorers found a dead world. There is no air and no water. Without an atmosphere, the sky is black at midday and temperatures swing by hundreds of degrees from day to night. No rivers or oceans have eroded the surface; no volcanoes are rebuilding the boring landscape.

The surface has survived unchanged for billions of years. Smooth plains are lava flows that froze on the Moon long before life arose on the Earth. Elsewhere, the Moon still bears the scars of every rock that has hit it from space, both large and small. The footprints of the visiting astronauts will survive for millions of years.

CRASH AND SPLASH

Astronomers now believe the Moon is the remains of a giant cosmic traffic accident. In its very early days, the Earth was hit by a runaway planet the size of Mars. White-hot molten rocks were splashed into space, and solidified into a ring of rocks around the Earth. These then came together to make up the Moon.

ICE ON THE MOON

Circling over the Moon's poles in 1998, the American Lunar Prospector spacecraft discovered patches of ice within some deep craters, where it is always shaded from the Sun, so the ice never melts or evaporates. Future manned expeditions could melt the ice into water, for drinking, washing and turning into rocket-fuel: there is enough ice to make a lake 10km across and 10m deep.

Prospecting spaceprobes such as the American Clementine are checking out the Moon from orbit, looking for sites where future astronauts could mine useful rocks, perhaps even extracting oxygen from them.

Twelve Apollo astronauts landed *on the Moon in these spider-shaped craft between 1969 and 1972 – and all of them returned safely to Earth. They brought back one-third of a tonne of Moonrocks, most of which are still locked away in a NASA vault.*

Although the Moon is smaller *than Earth, it is closer in size to its planet than almost any other moon we know. From space, you would see the two worlds orbiting each other as if they are a "double planet".*

Mars from Orbit

Through a telescope, Mars looks like a second Earth – but spaceprobes have revealed a surprisingly hostile place.

In 1877, an Italian astronomer called Giovanni Schiaparelli astounded the world of science with the discovery of "canals" on Mars. He claimed to see dark straight lines crossing the red deserts of this neighbouring world. They looked so artificial that they had to be made by intelligent creatures – the famous Martians.

At the time it seemed reasonable. Mars is a very Earth-like world. It is not much further from the Sun, and has a day almost the same as ours – just over 24 hours long. Mars has white icy polar caps which come and go with the seasons, and dark markings in the deserts that show seasonal changes.

Until the 1960s, some astronomers thought that these markings were vegetation growing in the spring and then dying back. But the first spacecraft to visit Mars, *Mariner 4*, found a very different world when it arrived in 1964. The atmosphere is made of unbreathable carbon dioxide, and it is incredibly thin – a hundred times thinner than the Earth's air. Mars's atmospheric blanket cannot retain much heat, so even on a summer's day the temperature barely rises above freezing.

The white polar cap is made partly of ordinary ice, joined in winter by carbon dioxide ("dry ice"). The temperature drops so low here that a third of the carbon dioxide "air" freezes in the winter.

The markings have turned out to be dark rocks that are covered and then uncovered by bright desert sand, blown by winds that change with the seasons. And the spacecraft orbiting Mars have found no signs of Schiaparelli's famous canals: they were simply an optical illusion.

POTATO MOONS

Mars has two tiny moons, which are probably asteroids captured by the Red Planet's gravity. Because Mars is named after the god of war, its moons are called Phobos ("fear" in Greek) and Deimos ("panic"). Both are shaped like potatoes. Phobos is 27km long, and Deimos is about half that size. Phobos is in a very low orbit, and will eventually crash into Mars – blasting out a new crater 300km across.

The Mars Global Surveyor spacecraft, which arrived at Mars in 1997, followed a long line of American and Russian probes that took bird's-eye views of the Red Planet. As well as taking pictures, the spaceprobe checked the nature of the rocks below the surface, looking for possible landing sites for other probes and, eventually, manned missions to Mars.

Mars

Deep canyons and vast volcanoes suggest that Mars enjoyed an exciting past, and long ago it may even have blossomed with life.

Spaceprobes have surveyed Mars so thoroughly that we now understand its surface better than we know some parts of the Earth! Three unmanned spacecraft have successfully landed and sent back close-up views of its rocky red deserts.

The first Mars missions scanned the planet's southern hemisphere and revealed a surface scarred with craters. The largest was 1,500km across – as big as the Caribbean Sea. Later probes found its northern hemisphere is very different, covered with smooth plains.

Towering up from these plains are huge volcanoes, now extinct. One place, an area the size of North America, has bulged upwards, cracking the surface to form the immense canyon of *Valles Marineris*.

MARTIAN RIVERS

The most surprising discovery was smaller meandering channels that look just like the beds of rivers that have dried up. Rivers cannot flow on Mars today. It's so cold that water would freeze to ice. And the air is so thin that if the ice melted, the water would quickly evaporate away. So the dried-up river beds suggest that Mars was once warmer and had a thicker atmosphere.

When Mars was warm and wet, it's quite likely that life began – just as it did on the early Earth. It probably developed only to microscopic cells, like bacteria or yeast, before the planet froze. Leading astronomers hope that some of these cells – or their fossils – may survive in the Martian soil.

A WATERY PAST

Astronomers now think that its giant volcanoes cloaked the planet in a dense atmosphere. These gases trapped the Sun's heat, so Mars was warm enough for rivers to flow. There were probably lakes, and possibly seas. But the planet's low gravity could not hold on to the dense atmosphere, and most of it leaked away into space to leave the frozen surface we see today.

Two Viking craft landed on Mars in 1976. Robot arms scooped up soil and tested it for signs of life in a tiny onboard laboratory. The results were negative.

But excitement soared in 1996, when scientists analysed a meteorite found in Antarctica. Traces of gas matched exactly with Mars's atmosphere, showing that this rock had been blasted out of the Red Planet's surface. Within the meteorite were tiny "rock-worms", looking just like fossilised bacteria.

Mars is only half the size of the Earth, yet its biggest volcano, Olympus Mons, is three times the height of Mount Everest and wide enough to cover the whole of Spain. It has been extinct for 100 million years. Sometimes it disappears from view in giant dust storms that can grow to envelop the whole planet.

The largest canyon on Mars, Valles Marineris, is so deep and wide that you could fit the whole of the Alps inside and still have room to spare. This giant crack in the planet's surface was named after the spaceprobe Mariner 9, first to go into orbit around Mars in 1971.

Asteroids

Cosmic rubble litters the void in space between Mars and
Jupiter – fragments of a planet that was never formed.

There's a big gap beyond the orbit of Mars,
before we come to the next planet, Jupiter. It's
almost as though there is a planet missing. But
astronomers reckon there could be about a
million small bodies in the "asteroid belt"
between Mars and Jupiter.

The asteroids are so small that even the most
powerful Earth-based telescope shows them as
little more than just points of light. Our first
close-up views came in 1991, when the
spaceprobe *Galileo* sped through the asteroid belt
on its way to Jupiter. Its pictures of Gaspra
showed this asteroid is not spherical but
potato-shaped, while Ida is long and thin with a
tiny "moon-asteroid" circling it.

BIRTH OF THE ASTEROID BELT

In the last century, many scientists thought that
the asteroids were the remains of a world that
had blown apart. Now, astronomers think exactly
the opposite. This cosmic rubble represents the
building-blocks of a planet that never formed.

When the Sun was born, it was surrounded by
a vast spinning disc stretching out beyond the
present orbit of Pluto. The disc was made of gas,
peppered with tiny specks of ice and rock, which
astronomers call "dust". This gradually grew into
solid worlds a few kilometres across, and these
came together to build up planets like the Earth.
But in the zone just inside Jupiter's orbit, the
giant planet's gravity kept stirring up these small
worlds. Prevented from accumulating into a
planet, the small primitive worlds have survived
to this day as asteroids. Some asteroids have
pale rocky surfaces, such as Vesta, which shines
more brightly than Ceres though only half its size.
On the other hand, Scheila is as black as coal, and
is probably covered with dark soot or tar.

In close-up, an asteroid *looks like a diseased potato, pitted with craters where smaller pieces of debris have crashed into its surface. The gravity of a small asteroid is not strong enough to pull it into a round ball, so it can have a weird shape.*

Over billions of years, *asteroids have frequently collided. Sometimes they smash each other apart; sometimes they stick together. In 1997 the Hubble telescope discovered a hole on Vesta that was 12km deep and 460km wide – and the asteroid measures only 530km across in total!*

DISCOVERY

Ceres was the first to be discovered – in 1801 by Italian astronomer Giuseppe Piazzi. At 950km across it is by far the biggest asteroid, yet still far smaller than any of the nine planets. Since then, astronomers have catalogued 7,000 asteroids. Even put together, they would make a world only one-third the size of the Moon.

The discoverer has the right to name the new asteroid. At first, they were given names from mythology, but in this century astronomers have called asteroids after cities, airlines and – in one case – a pet cat!

An asteroid's gravity *is so weak that if you stood on its surface you could escape into space just by jumping upwards!*

27

Jupiter

A colossal ball of liquid, Jupiter acts like a giant magnet and traps radiation from the Sun.

Imagine you could travel *into Jupiter further than Galileo's probe. After the clouds, you'd descend to a region where gases are compressed as densely as water. Further on, the gas behaves as a liquid metal (like mercury) and generates powerful magnetism. At the centre, you might find a core of molten rock with a temperature of 30,000°C – five times hotter than the surface of the Sun.*

Jupiter is the undisputed king of the planets. It's by far the biggest world circling the Sun – so huge that you could put all the other planets inside Jupiter and still have room to spare. In fact, Jupiter could accommodate no less than 1,300 Earths.

Despite its vast girth, Jupiter spins more quickly than any other planet. A day on Jupiter lasts just under 10 hours. This rapid spin makes the planet bulge outwards at its equator, so its shape is more like a tangerine than a ball.

Jupiter is very different from Earth and the other inner planets because it has no solid surface. It's made almost entirely from gases such as hydrogen, helium, ammonia and hydrogen cyanide. These are all unbreathable for humans, and some are downright lethal!

Blazing the trail to find out about Jupiter was *Pioneer 10*, the first probe to travel through the dangerous asteroid belt. It passed Jupiter in 1972, followed a year later by *Pioneer 11*. Two *Voyager* craft sped by Jupiter in 1979, taking much more detailed pictures of the swirling clouds, its moons and a thin ring around the planet.

Floating at the top of Jupiter's atmosphere is a gaudy array of coloured clouds. When Voyager 1 passed by in 1979, it sent back stunning video sequences of these clouds being whipped round the planet by fierce winds.

Between the bands of cloud lies Jupiter's Great Red Spot. This is a huge storm, three times the size of Earth, already raging for about 300 years.

Fragments of comet Shoemaker-Levy-9 smashed into Jupiter in 1994. Each impact blasted out a huge fireball, which erupted thousands of kilometres into space. The debris crashed back on to Jupiter's cloud-tops, creating dark "black eyes", each larger than the Earth. The Hubble Space Telescope observed these black eyes for months afterwards.

Five robot spacecraft have surveyed Jupiter in close-up. Sunlight out here is too dim to power solar panels, so each had to generate electricity in a miniature nuclear reactor.

THE GALILEO PROBE

In 1995 the *Galileo* spacecraft became the first artificial satellite of Jupiter. While previous missions had rushed past, sending back only a few snapshots, *Galileo* went into orbit around the giant planet and sent back pictures for many years.

Galileo's journey took six years. First it swung past Venus, then twice past the Earth, each time picking up extra speed from the planet's gravity. The NASA team was worried when *Galileo's* big antenna, which was furled up like a big umbrella, refused to open. They later found that messages could be sent successfully to and from *Galileo's* smaller antennae.

On its way, *Galileo* sent back the first close-up pictures of two asteroids. The spacecraft has photographed Jupiter's big moons and has discovered the first magnetised moons.

The Galileo spacecraft dropped a small probe into Jupiter's clouds. It was buffeted by fierce winds before it was crushed out of existence by Jupiter's enormous atmospheric pressure.

Jupiter's Family

Worlds of ice and fire, the moons orbiting giant Jupiter are some of the most fascinating objects in the Solar System.

Mighty Jupiter is the hub of a miniature Solar System – its family of 16 assorted moons. Indeed, four of the moons rival some of the planets in size and the biggest, Ganymede, is larger than both Mercury and Pluto.

In 1979, the two *Voyager* spacecraft sent back close-up pictures which astounded scientists. They showed that the four large moons are all totally different. Ganymede has huge grooves, while its neighbour Callisto (located outside the radiation belts) is covered in craters. Europa is smooth and dazzlingly white, but orange Io has erupting volcanoes.

LIFE ON EUROPA?

Europa is the most exciting of Jupiter's moons. *Voyager 1* discovered that it is brilliantly white and as smooth as a billiard ball. Astronomers believe that Europa was once covered by a watery ocean, which froze to ice when exposed to the cold of space.

The *Galileo* spacecraft has revealed fine cracks in the ice, suggesting that it's only a thin layer still covering an ocean of liquid water beneath. Some scientists think that this hidden ocean may well be the home for some kind of fishy alien lifeforms.

Liquid water could well up through cracks in Europa's icy crust.

Moons orbit Jupiter within a magnetic field 20,000 times stronger than the Earth's magnetism. The intense radiation would instantly kill a visiting astronaut.

The Italian astronomer *Galileo* discovered four of Jupiter's 16 moons as long ago as 1610: Ganymede, Callisto, Io and Europa.

Io

GALILEO PROBE

Blotchy orange Io looks at first sight like a cosmic pizza! Its surface is covered with brightly coloured sulphur compounds from volcanoes that erupt gas 300km into space.

Strange ridges stretch for thousands of kilometres across Europa's icy surface.

Saturn

The interplanetary tourist attraction of the 21st century may well be the glorious glittering rings of Saturn.

Saturn has many claims to fame. It is the most distant planet visible to the naked eye, the second-largest planet and the planet with the largest family of moons. Yet these facts all pale into insignificance when faced with the beauty of its unique set of rings.

Saturn is nine times wider than the Earth, and – like Jupiter – it's a gas giant without a solid surface. The gases making up Saturn are so thin that the planet has a very low density: Saturn would float in water if you could find an ocean big enough! This planet shows none of the gaudy cloud colours we see on Jupiter. The clouds are usually hidden by a layer of haze high in Saturn's atmosphere.

When the two *Voyager* spacecraft passed Saturn in 1980 and 1981, their cameras picked out clouds below the haze, and found they were being blown by hurricane force winds. Every 30 years or so, a giant storm erupts right up to the level of the haze, and we see a huge white cloud that gradually spreads around the planet.

This icy moon of Saturn, Mimas, bears a huge crater where it has been struck by a meteorite or small comet. Another moon has been broken in two by such a collision, while the famous rings are probably the debris of a shattered moon.

When *Voyager 1* skimmed past Saturn in 1980, its cameras could not see individual chunks, but could see the ringlets that the chunks form. Within each ringlet the icy chunks are following each other nose-to-tail.

Ice in space is gradually tarnished by radiation. The brightness of Saturn's rings means they are quite fresh and must have formed only 100 million years ago – a small fraction of Saturn's age. They may be the debris of a moon that was smashed apart by a collision with a passing comet.

RINGS OF ICE

Although Uranus and Neptune both have narrow dark rings, nothing can upstage Saturn's broad and brilliant set of rings. They are so wide that they would stretch two-thirds of the way from the Earth to the Moon. Yet they are less than a kilometre thick. If you made a scale model of the rings the thickness of ordinary paper, they would be wider than a house!

The rings are brilliant because they are made of ice. They are not solid, but are made of billions of icy chunks, ranging in size from snowballs to icebergs, each orbiting Saturn.

The Voyager spacecraft found that the rings are split into about 100,000 narrow ringlets. The larger gaps are caused by the gravity of Saturn's moons pulling on the ring particles.

Saturn's Family

The largest family of moons in the Solar System includes the most tantalising world so far unexplored by people.

This is the view we might get from Saturn's largest moon Titan. It is one of the biggest moons in the Solar System, and the only moon with a significant amount of atmosphere. Its "air" is twice as dense as Earth's atmosphere and, like ours, is made up mainly of nitrogen.

High in Titan's atmosphere is a layer of orange clouds. When *Voyager 1* zoomed past Titan in 1980, its cameras could not see down through the clouds to the surface below. (In this illustration, we are imagining a clearing in the clouds when we look upwards.) The clouds are probably made of "organic molecules" – substances similar to the chemicals that make up life.

Chilly lakes may lie in hollows on Titan's orange surface. Astronomers using radar to penetrate Titan's clouds (see Venus p14) have found there are patches on Titan which are highly smooth and shiny, suggesting a liquid surface. This far from the Sun, water is frozen to ice. But we could find lakes or even seas made of liquid ethane and methane, like the liquid natural gas used as a fuel on Earth.

Astronomers have detected signs of mountains on Titan, by observing wavelengths of light that can struggle out through the clouds. Could they be volcanoes?

Scientists think that life on Earth started from molecules like these. They dissolved in pools of water, and then gradually formed into living cells. But Titan is so far from the Sun that its temperature never rises above minus 180°C, so all its water is frozen into ice. Titan is like an early version of Earth in the deep freeze.

We'll find out what the surface of Titan is really like in 2004, when a European spaceprobe called *Huygens* plummets down through the clouds. It is going to be carried there by an American craft called *Cassini*, which will enter orbit around Saturn.

At the moment, our best guess is that the surface is coated with orange gunge that has drizzled down from the clouds high above. There may be seas of liquefied gas and high mountains – and these could be warmth-giving volcanoes.

Most of Saturn's 18 or so moons are bright balls of pure ice, pockmarked with numerous craters. Some of the smaller moons close to the planet act as "shepherds", herding up the particles that make up Saturn's rings. The moon Enceladus probably has "ice volcanoes", spouting water into space. Iapetus is bright on one side and dark on the other. And the flattened moon Hyperion is shaped like a hamburger, tumbling wildly as it circles Saturn.

Uranus

Tipped on its side, Uranus has thin dark rings and a moon, Miranda, with spectacular landscapes.

Uranus is four times wider than the Earth, yet it lies so far away you can hardly see it. No one knew Uranus existed until 1781, when an amateur astronomer, William Herschel, happened to point his telescope towards it. He wanted to call the new planet "George", after the English King.

Apart from its five biggest moons, little was known about Uranus until 1986, when *Voyager 2* swept past. It sent back the first pictures of Uranus's dark rings, and discovered ten new moons. In 1998 astronomers on Earth found two moons further out, bringing the total to 17 moons.

THE LONGEST YEAR

Uranus is the only planet that is tipped over, so that it orbits the Sun "on its side". As a result, the seasons are very odd indeed. Uranus takes 84 years to complete one "year". For half this time, the northern hemisphere is facing the Sun: at "midsummer", the Sun appears overhead at its north pole! For the next 42 years, the northern hemisphere is in darkness.

Astronomers think Uranus was knocked on its side by a small icy planet that smashed into it as the planet was born.

Miranda's surface is etched with deep grooves making vast oval shapes. Some astronomers think this moon was blasted apart by a comet. As Miranda reassembled from the pieces, each was squeezed to an oval.

Miranda, the small moon of Uranus, has amazing landforms. The cliffs tower to 20,000m. If we had cliffs on Earth on this relative scale, they would reach as high as the orbit of the Space Shuttle!

When *Voyager 2* zoomed past Uranus in 1986 it had already been travelling through space for nine years!

VOYAGER 2

Astronomers call Uranus "the most boring planet"! Even close-up pictures from Voyager 2 show just a plain blue-green globe, with a couple of very faint clouds.

Uranus is made mainly of water: there's a small rocky core at its centre, and the surrounding atmosphere is composed of hydrogen, helium and methane gases.

Eleven thin rings circle Uranus. Unlike the brilliant rings of Saturn, Uranus's rings are narrow and dark.

Neptune

The windiest planet is accompanied by a bizarre volcanic moon.

The blue planet Neptune is seen here from above the largest of its eight moons, Triton. Until *Voyager 2* flew past in 1989, astronomers knew hardly anything about these two worlds. They are so far from the Sun you need a telescope to see them at all.

Neptune was tracked down by the power of the human mind. Astronomers in England and France realised that Uranus was being pulled by the gravity of a planet further out, and calculated where that planet must lie. In 1846 it was discovered (at precisely that position) by astronomers in Berlin.

TWINS AND SPINS

Neptune is the twin of Uranus in size, and is also made mainly of water. But *Voyager 2* found that Neptune is much more interesting to look at: it has white clouds and large dark storms. The spacecraft found six new moons orbiting Neptune, in addition to the two already discovered from Earth.

Even more exciting than Neptune itself is its largest moon, Triton. Even before *Voyager*, astronomers were intrigued that it orbits Neptune in the opposite direction to Neptune's own spin. It was probably once a separate planet, like Pluto, which was captured by Neptune in a traumatic event that melted its surface.

Weird shapes were found on Triton's surface by Voyager. *These included long double ridges and "dimples", both of which are unique. Triton has a thin atmosphere – and pink frozen icecaps at its poles.*

Triton's biggest surprise was its sooty volcanoes, erupting from the coldest surface we know about in the Solar System. Voyager 2 *discovered dozens of dark volcanic plumes rising 8,000m like the smoke from a chimney. At that height, winds in Triton's tenuous atmosphere blow the smoke for over 100km.*

THE BLUE PLANET

Neptune sports three thin dark rings. Its blue atmosphere has streaks of white cloud, like the Earth's cirrus clouds ("mare's tails"). It's so cold here that the clouds are made of frozen methane (natural gas). *Voyager 2* found that the clouds were blown by the most powerful winds in the Solar System – ten times stronger than hurricane force on Earth. There was also a large dark spot, looking like Jupiter's Great Red Spot. But when the Hubble Space Telescope looked at Neptune several years later, the Great Dark Spot had mysteriously disappeared.

Pluto

The most distant planet from the Sun is also the weirdest.
In fact it may not even be a planet at all, but an "ice dwarf".

No one suspected Pluto existed until 1930, when the American astronomer Clyde Tombaugh discovered a faint speck of light out beyond Neptune. Then the surprises began to appear.

First, Pluto follows a very elongated path rather than a neat circle around the Sun. Its orbit crosses over Neptune's more circular route, so that sometimes (such as the period 1977 to 1999) Pluto is actually closer to the Sun than Neptune. Its orbit is also tilted up more than any other planet.

DOUBLE PLANET

With better telescopes, astronomers found that Pluto is far smaller than any other planet – only half the size of Mercury. And it's not alone. In 1978, a moon was discovered orbiting very close to Pluto itself: only a powerful telescope can show them apart. This moon, Charon, is half Pluto's own size, so that the two look more like a double planet than a planet and its moon.

Charon lies so close to Pluto that it looms large in the sky. Pluto and Charon always turn the same face to each other as they orbit: from one side of Pluto Charon is always visible, while an imaginary inhabitant on the other side would never see Charon at all.

In the 1990s, astronomers started finding many smaller worlds orbiting the Sun in this region, rather like the asteroid belt further in. Because they are made mainly of frozen water and gases, they are called "ice dwarfs".

Many astronomers now regard Pluto not as a true planet, but merely as the king of the ice dwarfs.

Charon is so close to *Pluto that it looks six times bigger in the sky than our Moon appears from Earth. It is drab grey in colour, while Pluto has a reddish-brown surface speckled with bright patches of ice.*

This far out in *space, the Sun looks like little more than a bright star.*

Comets

The spectacular tail of a comet, millions of kilometres long, is the work of a tiny dark visitor from the beyond.

Every few years, we are treated to the most glorious of all astronomical sights: the glowing dagger shape of a comet hanging in the twilight sky. From ancient times, people feared comets, but now we know they are merely celestial nomads – giant chunks of ice wandering in from the vast region beyond the planets.

The icy nature of comets was proved in 1986, when the European spaceprobe *Giotto* ran the gauntlet of Halley's Comet. As it penetrated into the great cloud of gas that forms the comet's head, *Giotto* was sandblasted by tiny grains of dust travelling at such speed that each carried the punch of a rifle bullet.

REVEALING THE SECRET

Fortunately the protective shield on *Giotto's* front saved it on the inward journey. Its camera sent back the first pictures (and so far the only ones) of the heart of a comet, before the dust onslaught destroyed the camera and *Giotto* limped into space. The secret was out: a comet is a lump of ice, spouting jets of steam as it is heated by the Sun.

The nucleus of Halley's Comet was revealed by the spaceprobe Giotto *to be a dark lump of ice only 16km long and 8km wide. On its sunlit side, spouts of steam erupt far out into space.*

WANDERERS IN TIME AND SPACE

A comet nucleus is a relic from the birth of the Solar System. Like asteroids, comets are leftover rubble, but they inhabit the icy regions way out beyond the planets. Every so often, one gets a "kick" which sends it in towards the Sun. The steam boiling off the heated cometary nucleus hides it inside a great glowing head of gases, laced with dust.

The Sun's energy drives away the outer parts of the comet's head, pushing the gas and dust off in two separate tails that can stretch for many millions of kilometres. After it has swept past the Sun, the comet's momentum carries it back to the dark and cold regions beyond the planets. It may be thousands of years before it returns to the vicinity of the Sun.

Comet Hale-Bopp was a brilliant sky-sight in 1997. Because it was discovered only two years earlier, astronomers had no time to send a spaceprobe there. But telescopes on the Earth found signs of 30 kinds of gas in its glowing head – including some of the gases that gave rise to life on Earth.

43

The Future

Over the last 50 years, unmanned spaceprobes have changed our view of our neighbours in space. From blurred globes seen through a telescope, the planets have now become worlds as real as the Earth.

Yet our exploration is only just starting. No spaceprobe has yet been to Pluto, and for most of the other planets we are still at Phase 1 – the stage where we are just sending spacecraft whizzing past a planet. Phase 2 involves sending a spaceprobe that stays in orbit, descends through the atmosphere, or lands. We have now reached that point with Venus, Mars and Jupiter.

LOOKING FOR CLUES

In the next few years, look out for future Phase 2 missions. Launched in October 1997, the *Cassini/Huygens* mission will investigate Saturn and its cloudy moon Titan. A spaceprobe will land on a comet, scoop up its ices and send them back in a cooled container. In these samples from the inter-planetary deep-freeze, scientists hope to find vital clues to the origin of the Solar System. "Landers" will dig rocks out of Mars and send them back to Earth for analysis, in the hope they may reveal the first definite signs of extra-terrestrial life. Another unmanned probe will smash through the icy surface of Jupiter's moon Europa, to explore the ocean underneath and check if any alien fish are living there.

New kinds of *rocket drive, like these nuclear electric propulsion units, are being developed to fly people to the planets.*

AD 2025: the first *manned expedition approaches Mars after a nine-month journey. The crew will spend six months on the Red Planet, searching patiently for any signs of past life, before they make the long return trip.*

FORWARD TO PHASE 3

But scientists and astronomers look forward most to Phase 3. That is when humans will visit the planets in person. So far, we've only extended Phase 3 to our nearest neighbour, the Moon.

The next target is Mars, the most Earth-like of the planets. American, Russian, European and Japanese scientists are already starting to plan a manned expedition to the Red Planet. They will eventually build a base there, using the Sun's energy to melt ice and to grow plants inside sealed greenhouses.

Hell-planet Venus may be off-limit to humans for ever, but astronauts could land on the poles of Mercury – and on the moons of Jupiter and the other "outer" planets. Indeed, one day we will *have* to make that trek.

Billions of years from now, the Sun will grow hotter in its old age. It will begin to scorch the Earth, and one day our descendants will be forced to live on Mars.

Later still, they will have to move to moons further out. Eventually, just before the Sun dies, people will undertake the ultimate space hop – across the depths of space to find a younger star with another welcoming planet like Earth.

Planetary Data

PLANET	Diameter at equator km and relative to Earth	Mass relative to Earth	Density relative to water	Average temperature °C	Tilt of axis
Mercury	4878 0.38	0.055	5.5	350 (day) 170 (night)	0°
Venus	**12,103 0.95**	**0.81**	**5.2**	**465**	**3°**
Earth	12,756 1.00	1.00	5.5	15	23°
Mars	**6786 0.53**	**0.11**	**3.9**	**-23**	**25°**
Jupiter	142,980 11.0	318	1.3	-150	3°
Saturn	**120,540 9.41**	**95**	**0.7**	**-180**	**27°**
Uranus	51,120 4.11	15	1.3	-210	83°
Neptune	**49,530 3.96**	**17**	**1.6**	**-220**	**28°**
Pluto	1170 0.18	0.002	2.1	-220	65°

[1] A.U.= Astronomical Unit, the distance of the Earth from the Sun.
[2] Relative to the stars. If the length of the "day" (sunrise to sunrise) is very different, it is given in brackets.

Average distance from Sun millions of km and A.U.[1]	Range in distance A.U.[1]	Period of revolution ("Year")	Period of rotation[2]	No. of known moons
57.9 0.387	0.31-0.47	88d	59d (176d)	0
108.2 0.723	**0.72-0.73**	**225d**	**243d (E to W) (117d)**	**0**
149.6 1.000	0.98-1.01	365d	23hr 56m (24hr)	1
227.9 1.523	**1.38-1.66**	**687d**	**24hr 37m**	**2**
778.3 5.202	4.95-5.45	11.9yr	9hr 55m	16
1427 9.539	**9.00-10.01**	**29.5yr**	**10hr 39m**	**18**
2871 19.19	18.28-20.08	84yr	17hr 14m (E to W)	17
4497 30.06	**29.79-30.33**	**165yr**	**16hr 7m**	**8**
5914 39.53	29.6-49.3	248yr	6d 9hr (E to W)	1

Planetary Firsts

1959	Luna 3	USSR	pictures of Moon's far side
1962	Mariner 2	US	flyby of another planet (Venus)
1965	Mariner 4	US	close-up pictures of Mars
1966	Luna 9	USSR	pictures from Moon's surface
1969	Apollo 11	US	manned landing on Moon
1971	Mariner 9	US	Mars-orbiter: pictures of volcanoes, canyons and dried-up river beds
1972	Landsat 1	US	optical and infrared views of Earth
1973	Pioneer 10	US	close-up pictures of Jupiter
1974	Mariner 10	US	close-up pictures of Venus and Mercury
1975	Veneras 9&10	USSR	Venus landers: pictures of surface
1976	Vikings 1&2	US	Mars-landers: pictures of surface and (unsuccessful) search for life
1978	Pioneer Venus	US	radar maps of Venus
1979	Voyagers 1&2	US	movie sequences of Jupiter: pictures of its moons, including active volcanoes on Io
1979	Pioneer 11	US	close-up pictures of Saturn
1980	Voyager 1	US	detailed views of Saturn, its rings and moons
1985	Vegas 1&2	USSR	balloons in Venus atmosphere
1986	Voyager 2	US	close-up pictures of Uranus
1986	Giotto	ESA*	detailed pictures of nucleus of Halley's Comet
1989	Voyager 2	US	close-up pictures of Neptune
1990	Hubble Space Telescope	US/ESA	detailed views of planets, including Pluto-Charon
1990	Magellan	US	detailed radar views of Venus
1991	Galileo	US	close-up pictures of an asteroid (Gaspra)
1994	Ulysses	ESA/US	flight over pole of the Sun
1994	Clementine	US	pictures of Moon's poles
1995	Galileo	US	probe into Jupiter's atmosphere; Jupiter-orbiter
1997	Mars Pathfinder	US	rover on Mars
1998	Lunar Prospector	US	detection of ice on Moon

*ESA=European Space Agency